I'M LISTENING, GOD
PSALM 19 FOR CHILDREN
BY ELSPETH CAMPBELL MURPHY
ILLUSTRATED BY JANE E. NELSON

I'M LISTENING, GOD
PSALM 19 FOR CHILDREN
BY ELSPETH CAMPBELL MURPHY
ILLUSTRATED BY JANE E. NELSON

I'M LISTENING, GOD
© 1983 Elspeth Campbell Murphy for the entire text and David C. Cook Publishing Co. for the illustrations.
All rights reserved. Except for brief excerpts for review purposes, no part of this book may be reproduced or used in any form without written permission from David C. Cook Publishing Co., Elgin, Illinois 60120. Printed in the United States of America
ISBN: 0-89191-583-4   LC: 81-71813

Do you know what, God?
Tonight I saw millions
　and billions
　and trillions
　of stars in the sky—more than I'd ever seen before.
We're on vacation, and I can see the sky a lot better
out here.

I tried to count the stars, but I lost track.

"Listen, listen," the sky seemed to say. "Somebody wonderful made me!"

"I'm listening," I answered—and then I laughed, because I was listening with my eyes.

Day after day your sky goes on talking without words. Night after night it tells about you, God.

"Listen, people everywhere," your sky seems to call. "Somebody wonderful made me."

When I look at your world, God, it's like you're telling me about yourself without using words.

And I want to listen. My mom says really listening to people shows how much we care about what they have to say.

I care about you, God.

My best friend and I can talk right now, even though she isn't here. We talk by writing letters. You talk to me with words, too, God. That's what the Bible is—you talking to me in a long,
    long,
        long letter.

Yesterday we went panning for gold, and guess what! I found a tiny gold nugget shining in the dirt.

Gold is valuable. But here's a riddle: what's more valuable than gold?

The Bible is! Because that's how you talk to me and tell me what you want for me.

You know how I like my pancakes, God? With lots and lots of sweet honey. Well, here's another riddle: what's sweeter than honey?

Your Word. Because that's how you talk to me and tell me that you love me. Listening to you makes me happy, God.

I hope the words I say and the thoughts I think will make you happy, too. Because you're my Friend—my strong and special Friend.